Ordinary Magic
(Little Vignettes from the Big Apple)

Lisa Hickman

Hickman & Company
New York, New York

Hickman & Company
New York, New York
www.lisahickman.com

Book Photos & Cover Design @2017 Mike Olivieri
Book Layout ©2017 BookDesignTemplates.com

Ordinary Magic (Little Vignettes from the Big Apple)/Lisa Hickman-- 1st ed.
ISBN 978-0692948545

FOR MY NIECES,
OLIVIA JUNE & VIOLET ANNABELLE,
WHO ARE EXTRAORDINARY IN THEIR MAGIC.

AUTHOR'S NOTE

I'm a glass-half-full kind of gal. Now, that doesn't mean I take to wearing rose-colored glasses when life gets tough. When Ugly appears, I simply remind myself that Beauty will return soon—she's probably just eating potato chips on her sofa in front of the TV or maybe she's trying on a new shade of red lipstick at Macy's makeup counter. Even Beauty needs down time now and then— not unlike you and me!

Ordinary Magic is a collection of stories involving tiny moments of unexpected beauty I experienced in New York City between 2012 and 2017. The collection celebrates my favorite beauty— the kind I've seen in strangers who've made me smile, laugh, or reflect suddenly on how glorious it really is to be a human being. These accidental collisions and conversations all have one thing in common: the hero is outlook— positive rather than negative,
or Beauty before Ugly, as it were.

These moments all occurred on seemingly occasion-less days. I'd be having a humdrum, what-am-I-here-for sort of moment and then something downright remarkable would abruptly happen in an elevator, taxi, or the middle of 10th Avenue— in the way an exceptional, unexplainable magic trick is pulled off. You never see it coming.

I wrote about these poignant little happenings and posted them on social media. The responses were enthusiastic — turns out everyone is looking to escape the mundane every now and then! Friends and family shared my stories, which made me think, well, hey, I should put these stories together in a book. And so here we are.

I hope you enjoy my adventures. I hope they remind you to keep looking for Beauty— there she is! Ready to paint even the grayest day red, like a lipstick kiss on a love letter.

Lisa Hickman   New York City   2017

ACKNOWLEDGEMENTS

We are partly who we are because of *who* we come from,
right? Someone who lived before you in your family liked to
bake apple pie and so do you. Someone was quick to anger
and so are you. Another was good at summersaults and so
are you. We all carry a piece of this, a scrap of that—
I celebrate my loved ones who were and are,
largely responsible for my spirit and outlook on life. Some of
the people below are directly connected with the production of
this book and others are not so directly connected, but
important nonetheless. Without all of these folks, without their
love, *Ordinary Magic* would not exist.
In them, I am me.

Robin Shepherd, my mother, makes things.
Clothes. Cakes. Pillows. Gardens. Strong Daughters. A
classic over-achiever, Mom, also a hospice nurse, taught me
that to pursue a dream, you must do it tirelessly and with
precision. The owner of my favorite laugh, she can also be
downright silly at times, but was super serious about giving
me the encouragement to complete *Ordinary Magic.*
It's a powerful thing when your
Mom thinks you can do anything, and if I can—
really it's mostly her fault.

James W. Shepherd, my step-father, edited this book. Jim is
a fabulous storyteller, which was fifty percent of the reason I
asked him to work on this project. He had the technical goods,
(after teaching English for thirty-one years,) but I also knew he
had the heart for the job. I couldn't have finished
Ordinary Magic without him—turns out,
Jim is as good an editor as he is a step-dad.

Mike Olivieri, my partner in love and a brilliant photographer, created the cover design and author shot for *Ordinary Magic*. Mike is more than my rock— in him I have a giant boulder, who listens, supports, and cheers for me in the littlest and biggest of ways. I'm constantly inspired by his compassion for others and lucky beyond measure to have found my soulmate in this talented man who makes my life way more fun.

Annabelle Wright, my Nana. Her kindness and strength have been as constant in my life as the night sky. That moon in her sky, would be my grandfather, **Lyle Wright,** who could accomplish more from sun-up to sun-down than anyone I've ever known. **Lyla Dyer,** another star in my life, is the perfect combination of aunt and friend. She and my uncle, **Ben Dyer,** are not only always there for me— they're also my favorite people to party with! **Lauren Hickman-Herling,** my sister, also stellar, excels at everything from being a Mom to a Broadway stage manager. I'm thankful every day that we're sisters and I hope someday when I grow up, I'll be a lot like her. I have a wild, wonderful extended family— big love to the **Geisberts, Gingells, Fouches, Stones, Wrights, Cooks, Ridges, Hickmans, Irizarrys, Herlings, Kearns, Bavaros, Sulsentis, Drulises,** and **Undurragas.**

Stephen Hickman, my father, taught me to follow my instincts, look for signs, and to dream. He lived to make us laugh and I miss him so much, I can't take his name out of my cell phone. Do you hear that distant, "Hey, ya'll! That's my Lis-ee!"? That's Big Daddy Hickman celebrating the completion of *Ordinary Magic*— knockin' back Modelos in his cowboy hat from his big leather recliner in heaven.

I'm surrounded by a terrific, talented group of friends, artists, mentors, colleagues, students, teachers, and collaborators of all ages who inspire me daily. I'm nothing without the people around me taking chances and making art.

I want to express gratitude for the first believers of *Ordinary Magic*— those friends who clicked "like" in social media land, those who asked if they could print my stories to cheer up sick family members or make coworkers laugh, those who inboxed me with words of encouragement to keep writing. Look what happens when you tell someone you believe in them! Let's do that more often.

Contents

"The world is full of magic things,
patiently waiting for our senses to grow sharper."

—W.B. YEATS

1 Born to Drive

When I jumped into a yellow cab this crisp October morning, a striking woman with long brown wavy hair and a smart black cap, asked me to fasten my seatbelt since it was her, "first day behind the wheel." Said she'd always dreamed of driving a cab, so on her fiftieth birthday she'd decided to leave her receptionist job and go after her dreams. It was quite literally, "time to push the pedal to the medal." I studied her as I fastened my seatbelt. She was super-tall, capable, strong looking, both hands placed carefully on the wheel, sporting pink driving gloves with the fingertips cut off, revealing shiny fuchsia nails. She smiled a lot as she talked and in the rearview mirror I kept catching her gold tooth flashing in the autumn light. It smelled like new beginnings in this cab, like the scent of brand new school clothes or a new backpack filled with fresh paper and newly sharpened pencils. Ah, the possibilities of an empty notebook! I could see all of that, feel all of that in her hopeful, excited grin. As we sailed down the FDR drive, I snapped to attention, noticing that we were actually speeding more than sailing. Once we got off the drive, she blew two red lights and almost hit a traffic cop. Even my finger tips were sweating. The ride was harrowing, but what a thrill—there's nothing more exciting (or dangerous!) than pursuing a dream. When the ride ended, I gave her a great tip and a loud, "Go GIRL!" I voiced a silent vow to keep accelerating my own dreams with delight and fervor like this woman, who knew there was no time to hit the brakes on what she wanted from life.

2 Cheese Curls and Dumb Bells

I'm going nowhere fast—numbly pedaling my stationary bike— when someone taps my elbow. It's the woman on the bike beside me, probably in her late seventies. She's rocking zebra-print workout gear, a peroxide 60's up-do, and black sunglasses. She pedals so slowly her legs don't even seem like they're moving. I'm only mildly surprised when she unzips her purple bedazzled fanny-pack and hands me a cheese curl. "I'm just here for the eye candy," she admits, arching a drawn-on eyebrow as she points to the man in front of us. I know you shouldn't accept candy from strangers, but a cheese curl from a grandmother type is all right... right?! Anyway, I'm devouring the cheese curl when I notice the aforementioned "eye candy"—an older shirtless man in a crooked toupee who's grinning and lifting tiny dumb bells in our direction, wearing neon green bike shorts, one size too small. I gasp as she throws me a conspiratorial wink and another cheese curl and we stifle giggles as we crunch, pedal, and "devour" the eye candy together.

3 Four Train Hocus-Pocus

Just as I sit down on the 4 express train to travel one stop, a short man with a long, thin black beard and tiny round dark sunglasses parks a baby carriage covered in red velvet and gold fringe directly in front of me. I watch as he pulls a live white dove from a tiny metal pot—which is of course, "empty" at first. Next he reveals a "blank" sketch book which becomes a full color collection of comics, and then there's an ordinary rope that transforms into an extraordinary silver cane— in the blink of an eye. The finale: what has to be nothing less than a thirty pound white rabbit, appears quite suddenly in a clear box, sniffing and staring at us with penetrating pink eyes. The magician never utters a word—not even a cheesy, "TA-DA!"—the only sounds in that train car are sudden exclamations of "WOAH!" and "COME ON!," from the passenger-audience. This guy is good. The four minute show-ride ends and I follow the magician off the train onto a platform that is unusually empty. He guides his magic carriage to the left and I'm walking behind him toward the exit stairs. Suddenly, I hear a commotion and loud voices to my right. I turn quickly, but mysteriously, there's nothing to see in that direction. I immediately turn back again to head up the stairs with the magician— only to find that he and his fringe-covered buggy have simply vanished. There's no elevator, no other trains have arrived to board, he's not at the top of the stairs— it would take time to launch a velvety stroller holding pots, rope, a dove, and a thirty pound rabbit up fourteen steps! Was this all just an illusion or will he pop out of my backpack with a loud, "ABRACADABRA!"? Whatever the case, it's my turn to shout an appreciative, "COME ON!," as I jog upstairs to start a day that will hopefully continue to thrill.

4 Grounds for Arrest

Anxious to get my day going, I drowned my Extra-Dark-Roast-100% Columbian coffee with cream and too much sugar before rushing out of my favorite deli on Broadway. I smiled at Jeannie the clerk as I cradled my coffee cup. This deli is immaculate, probably because Jeannie is always cheerfully wiping the already clean counter even cleaner. This is a woman who is bright and proud, not bored or angry like others I've met who work these thankless counter jobs. Jeannie is a star. She never forgets the napkin with the coffee or the straw for the soda. She doesn't use the calculator to make change, and even remembers your difficult sandwich order. Yes, that one. Well, this morning Jeannie seemed overly enthusiastic as I was leaving—she almost jumped over the shiny counter while waving her rag and saying my name. "She's always so nice," I thought as I waved back and ran to catch a cab that was slowing at the corner. "Must have a gymnastics background!," I thought smiling, as I sipped my morning brew. And then it dawned on me. I'd forgotten to pay for my coffee. Jeannie's Olympic-qualifying farewell vault wasn't a long good-bye. It was an Olympic effort to collect $1.25. I told you she was a star. I'll make amends for my caffeinated-crime tomorrow. I might even buy Jeannie a cup—just to let her know I'm a coffee thief with a conscience.

5 Bad Hair Day

Somewhere on 10th avenue, I'm trying to make good on a bad hair day by using a dusty, deserted storefront window as my mirror. The transition from bad to good will require a brush, a comb, and a few urgent pumps of high-volume, strong-hold, ultra-finishing hairspray. If you know me, you know these items are in my purse. This old corner shop closed years ago— they sold incense, tiny statues, love potions, hate potions, and concoctions to encourage well-behaved hair. But alas, I'm too late. Bad hair days rarely have good timing. A small old white-haired woman in a white housedress covered with small red tulips approaches from nowhere and watches as I discipline my bad hair with a little teasing and a lot of pumping. "I give up!" I say, shrugging and laughing. She smiles and responds in a thick unfamiliar accent, "Don't geeeeeeve up! You look in the mirror and I see bee-you-tee-full." Now, that's a good bad hair day.

6 Caught Blue Handed

These stretch jeans fit so perfectly in the dressing room—but now I'm on 14th street and the 98% spandex, 2% cotton "perfect fit jeans" are totally imperfect in the way they keep sliding lower and lower as I walk. I've been hiking them back up frequently, so now the "dark wash" has dyed my hands navy blue. I need a belt, fast. Eureka! I spot a street vendor. I see purses, socks, hats, sunglasses, earrings—and mangos? Whatever, as long as I can find a five dollar belt that fits, who cares if accessories and fruit are sold together? I wave a navy blue hand at the friendly looking vendor wearing a white visor and explain my need for an emergency belt. White Visor struggles to produce a tiny bright yellow belt from under the table, forcing me to wonder if someone under there may have been wearing it. He kindly holds up my coat while I wrestle, pull, and pray—but alas I cannot make that yellow plastic belt stretch two more inches—which of course makes me second guess the whole cupcakes-for-breakfast thing this morning. We try more belts and nothing works, but White Visor needs a sale and I need a belt and moments later a wide silver disco sort of belt surfaces—which is imperfect for this outfit, so of course it fits perfectly. I hastily press five bucks into his hand and shout, "You saved my life!" I have to hustle to make it to rehearsal so I'm threading the four inch wide disco belt through three inch jean loops while texting and balancing my ever-present, over-sized purse. I rush to the corner to cross the street. Suddenly, a hand grabs the back of my coat, pulling me back quickly, just as the M14 bus whizzes by, honking. "You saved my life!," I hear myself saying again— this time to a young dude wearing wide green eyeliner and a smile even wider. I point to his eyes and blurt out, "I like that green eyeliner." He replies, "I like your blue hands," and we both laugh. Feeling doubly lucky, I'm still all smiles as I safely cross the street, knowing full well the lesson here is, "It's better to be caught blue-handed with your stretch jeans down than to get hit by a bus."

7 Breath-Stroke

On Monday nights I share a swim lane with a really spicy New Yorker named Flora. Despite our thirty year age difference, we have lots in common. Between pounding out laps, we discuss movies, the guy doing the butterfly in lane three, and any salty one-liners we've delivered during the week. Plenty of folks are training for big things in this pool — but no one ever bugs us to pick up the pace when Flora and I take chat breaks in the corner of our lane. Is this because I'm so tough they don't mess with her, or because she's so tough they don't mess with me? We'll never know. What's clear is we've got a good thing going. Swimming with Flora starts my week off right. Tonight I got out of the pool and Flora shouted over the splashing of lane three's butterfly marathon, "Lisa! You look like you're feeling RIGHTEOUS!" And that was exactly how I felt.

8 Be Good Now

I'm debating about whether or not to buy these chocolate cupcakes while waiting in a long line at the corner store on 11th and Avenue C. This place is happening! In the center of the store there's a man resembling a whistling John Wayne attacking his scratch-off game with a nickel, while a hipster looking couple behind me has a loud, "she-said-he-said" sort of "conversation" about the difference between winking and blinking when a beautiful blonde walks past you to get to the detergent aisle. The woman at the register is picking at her silvery nail instead of ringing the next customer up in a timely way. We're all lost in our own business when John Wayne yells, "BE GOOD, NOW!" Everyone stops. What is the meaning of this message? Who is it for? Is it an expectant prayer for the scratch-off? Therapy for the troubled hipsters? A Health Department warning for Nail Picker at the register? Poignantly timed nutritional advice for me since I'd been squeezing this package of cupcakes for five minutes? Or was it a general overall sort of life announcement for everyone in the corner store? Whatever it's intended meaning, we all interpret the phrase: The hipsters stop arguing. Nail Picker rolls her eyes, stops picking at her nail, and turns up the radio. I put the cupcakes back. And John Wayne lets out a whoop and shakes his scratch-off in the air, joining us in line to collect his winnings.

9 Dame Jameson

An actress, theatre-famous in her day, comes into
the restaurant where I work every week. Now, I
don't adore her just because she leaves fifty
percent of the bill as a tip every time. And I don't
think she's cool just because she throws down at
least two Jameson shots every time either. She's
my kind of woman simply because, well into her
nineties, she's still acting. She may not be able to
power her own wheelchair, and, all right, her
companion cuts her food— but this dame can still
throw down a whiskey with the best of them and
make you smile with a Shakespeare sonnet. I am
completely mesmerized by every little movement
she makes. Every time I see her, I always bow
slightly when she rolls through the door. She gets a
kick out of this and returns the honor with a big grin
and a spirited wink— I imagine she's sending me
this message, every time: "Do what you love and
you will live forever."

10 A Perfect Fit

I went to the store to buy a dress for my niece but
on my way back from the children's section, I
spotted a wild floor length leopard print skirt, which
looked like it would Fit Me Perfectly. As I ap-
proached the rack, I honestly wasn't sure whether
the voice I heard shrieking, "Don't Buy Another
Leopard Print Item!," was a voice in my head or the
voice of a concerned store associate making an
announcement directly to me on the overhead PA
system. Had I been seen here before—wearing and
buying all things leopard print? I ignored the voice
and proceeded to the register, glancing lovingly at
the leopard print skirt now on top of the other items
piled in my arms. As the cashier scanned the tags, I
began to feel extreme pre-buyer's remorse—how
many articles of animal print clothing did I already
own? Thirty? No. Forty? Worried that my friends
were going to start thinking I may be anticipating a
move to the jungle, I sadly asked the cashier to re-
move the beloved skirt from my pile of purchases.
"I'm not gonna do it," I said, and the cashier nodded
in agreement, carelessly snatching the skirt quickly
out of the bag and tossing it behind her. It landed

on the Back Counter—you know, the sad place where items that were once carried as carefully as one might carry a leopard print child are suddenly scrapped without a second thought. That counter. I couldn't take my eyes off that precious skirt— now partially covering a pair of neon green roller blades. It even looked good with those! Had I made an enormous mistake? What had I done in not doing? As I stared at the leopard print skirt, (now just a lonely discard,) the cashier leaned forward and said, "Yeah, good idea. The skirt? Just a little Too Crazy." Without missing a beat, I leaned forward and whispered urgently, "Could you add it back on? I knew it would Fit Me Perfectly."

11 Pig-Tailed Pro

I just auditioned for "Mom" with a terrific freckled seven year old wearing a huge smile and lots of pink. We knew the lines perfectly, but in the room, "Daughter" went up on a line during our second take. I ad-libbed to cover and when she realized this, she screamed suddenly and then began giggling uncontrollably. Of course, giggles are contagious and once I started snort-laughing, the casting director also doubled over in laughter. None of this usually happens— which explains that unusual electricity in the room, the brightness of three strangers sharing joy in a single moment. We agreed to take one more just as my pig-tailed scene partner—wise beyond her years—cheerfully shrieked, "Mistakes are OK!" So we danced the giggles out and did another take and it was perfect.

12 Sometimes, You Just Wing It

Thirsty and on the run, I jumped into a yellow cab and quickly opened my extra large bottle of seltzer water, immediately drenching myself and the entire floor-to-ceiling of the cab. Thankfully, the cab driver stayed dry behind the plastic divider, but as he took the next street super-fast I sorta panicked, wondering if he was annoyed about the carbonated conundrum. Soaking in soda and shame, I threw open my purse and grabbed the first thing I found— a giant maxi-pad—which I hastily began using to "absorb" the results of my bubbly water explosion. I was still detailing the plastic divider with the maxi-pad wings (!) when the cab stopped at what was certain to be my significantly dryer destination. As I sheepishly handed him soggy cash, the cab driver tapped his head, pointed at the water-logged maxi in my hand and laugh-yelled in a thick Russian accent, "Very inventive! That is why women rule the world!" "I'm glad you know it!," I yelled-laughed back, and as I got out of the cab, I flashed him a big smile and waved goodbye with the dripping maxi— water flying in all directions—much to the delight of a crowd waiting to cross on the corner of 23rd and 5th Avenue.

13 Elevator Shaft

I ran smack into an old foe today— in an elevator of all places. We squared off instantly, like cowboys ready to duel, each claiming our territory— one of us on the east side of the elevator, the other on the west. My hand went immediately for my hip at the sight of this bandit— but I remembered quickly that I was not wearing a holster or carrying a revolver. Before I could say, "This elevator ain't big enough for the both of us," the villain started nervously shoving handfuls of barbecue Fritos in his mouth. Nothing shuts down a showdown like Fritos crumbs dangling from your rival's chin. I don't know whether the hilarity of those lonesome Fritos stopped me dead in my tracks or whether I'm just gettin' a little softer—but I resisted the urge to engage in a good old-fashioned verbal shootout with the rascal. Who needs wild grudges and revenge duels? I shot the scoundrel a killer smile instead.

14 When Mercury is in Retrograde

When Mercury is in retrograde, everybody tuned
into the stars knows that most transportation and
communication goes to hell— which was bound to
make this post-snow February Friday in New York
City rather freaky. So when my bus stopped suddenly in the middle of the slushy street— just so
that I could get on without swimming through a wide
pond of melted-muck— I was all smiles. I skipped
up the bus steps and shouted, "Thanks man!," as
the Bus Driver nodded and said in a cool, booming
voice, "IT'S YOUR WORLD." I thought about that
possibility until we reached my stop. When I waved
goodbye, Bus Driver flashed a lovely gap-toothed
grin, which made me forget all about the cold during
my walk to the train station. Lucky again, I spotted a
seat on a packed 1 train, and as soon as I sat down
an old man with a white crew cut, wearing white
wire-rimmed glasses and icy-pink lipstick, began
blowing kisses at me. I tried not to react, but as the
kisses arrived more frequently, "MWAH! MWAH!
MWAH!"—I let out a tremendous belly laugh. Pink
Lips laughed back and said, "Take it easy, Miss
French Fry," which got everyone within earshot

belly laughing too. A few of the kiss witnesses were still giggling in my direction when we got off the train, and as I went my own way, a large clump of melting snow fell from the heavens, (or maybe just that traffic light on 79th Street,) and landed on my forehead. Surprised by the "sudden romance" of that giant icy-kiss, I ducked into a corner coffee shop to dry off and of course re-apply my mascara. After that, the only sensible thing to do was order an over-sized chocolate chip cookie and sit on a stool that was much too high for me in the front window where I could watch other New Yorkers dodging puddles and perhaps, kisses. I took a bite of the cookie and smiled. It wasn't even noon and already this frigid, freaky Friday had been full of sweet surprises—which could only mean that even when Mercury is in retrograde, it really is my world.

15 11th & Broadway

What's better than two brunette teenage girls, both in jeans and t-shirts, wearing the same yellow high-top sneakers on the corner of 11th and Broadway, spraying each other with pink silly-string and yelling, "Weirdo!" back and forth at the top of their lungs? Only the guy in a three-piece charcoal pin-striped suit who flew by me on a ratty skateboard, holding his briefcase above his head, smiling and shouting, "Late for a meeting!"

16 Birds of a Feather

A young man holding a hard hat with sawdust on his jeans, taps rapidly on the pet shop window on 14th and Avenue B, trying to get the attention of a beautiful yellow-green bird. He says, "You're my baby, baby!" over and over in a loud voice, while the bird remains motionless on a fake tree branch, presumably unimpressed by such poorly scripted overtures. As I'm watching Dusty Jeans go all coo-coo, a shiny red Cobra rolls up blasting, "Funky Cold Medina," and a dude with salt and pepper pork chop sideburns leans over his window, (which is half-up,) and says to me, "Come on baby, make my day." Now it's my turn to remain motionless while pondering badly composed come-ons—(this time a Doors lyric combined with a line from *Dirty Harry*.) The bird and I are sisters in stillness as Pork Chop Sideburns revs his engine and blows smoke from his Newport in my direction while Dusty Jeans throws down his hard hat and dances a circle around it on his toes, bowing wildly toward the bird. Would you believe me if I told you the yellow-green bird and I actually exchange a look and then an eye roll just as the two Romeos get the hint and dance/drive away? You should. You know what they say about birds of a feather.

17 Not As I Do

Today in the locker room at the gym, there was a little girl around five years old wearing a green swimsuit and cap with matching green goggles and flip-flops. Engaged in some serious shadow-boxing in the mirror, she gave a powerful, "UH!" with each punch. Her mother noticed me watching curiously and said, "Katie didn't want to swim today. She 'becomes' a super-hero named, 'Super-No,' when she's forced to do something she doesn't want to do. We don't know whether the acting classes are hurting or helping," she added, chuckling. "Oh, I'm sure they're helping!" I said quickly. "Acting classes really enriched my life." I flashed a reassuring smile, only to receive a strange look from the Mom as she hustled Katie to the pool. I shrugged and began squeezing into my swimsuit, mouth open— gritting my teeth, (like you do when you squeeze into a swimsuit), and then I caught my reflection in the mirror. Three of my teeth were still blocked out with black makeup from my dress rehearsal earlier in the day. You see, I was playing a filthy, scrappy street urchin in a George Bernard Shaw play and had dashed from rehearsal to make my weekly swim without removing the last of my "dirt." Poor Katie. Her mother was probably by the pool in a panic, using her phone to register Katie in Chess, Karate, Pottery and Knitting— filling her kindergarten schedule— with anything but acting class.

18 Perspiration Chaos

It's rush hour on this deeply humid August morning. I'm positively swimming through Union Square train station trying to keep my head above water in a pool of commuters flopping around me like fish. Feeling a steady stream of sweat flowing down my back, the thought, "Did I remember my deodorant?!," strikes me suddenly. As I nervously flounder to recall the answer, a few commuters throw me the old fish eye since my abrupt stillness has created something like the parting of the Red Sea. Had I applied deodorant this morning, somewhere between coffee and my seventeen minute search for house keys? I think about taking a quick whiff of my armpit, but worry I'd look up from this investigation to find an ex-boyfriend with a "That's no surprise," sort of look on his face since I'd always been bad at remembering the important things. Birthdays. Anniversaries. Deodorant. So I take a tiny sniff in that general direction, keeping my eyes up, and that's when I see a Preacher Man up ahead, shouting into a microphone about mayhem. Preacher Man's eyes lock on mine as he yells, "Your actions will cause condemnation!" Then he throws one arm in the air and screams, "Renounce your SINS!" Surely this is a sign. Preacher Man knows my secret. (Or rather, he knows I *forgot* my Secret.) Since I've always been a devout believer in avoiding catastrophe and am not so big on sin, instead of going directly to work, I hurry to the closest pharmacy instead— to purchase a little redemption.

19 Va Va Va Vroooom

This morning, I found forty bucks on the sidewalk, treated myself to a cab to work, and then left my cell phone in the cab. Since my ringtone is the sound of a motorcycle revving, (I like motorcycles,) I imagined the cabbie driving around for hours without recognizing the motorcycle sound as a ringtone— totally freaked out by being tailed by a phantom motorcyclist. Imagine my joy when in under an hour, Cool Cabbie answered my phone and drove up to my restaurant gig, grinning ear to ear. Was that a reward-anticipating gleam in his eye, pure kindness, or had he browsed through the pictures on my phone? Knowing I would never know, I pressed some cash into his hand and gave him a "high five" anyway. I was down forty bucks between the cab ride and the cell phone bounty, but I *did* find that forty bucks this morning, so it felt like I was ahead— or at least—even. Chuckling over the unlikely evenness of things, I'm back in the dining room and the customers are eating lunch while I'm visualizing the lottery numbers I'll play tonight. I've got luck, not blood, pumping through these veins! I'm invincible, practically skipping through the restaurant doing jazz hands, when I accidentally bump into a glass of ice— which spills all over the crotch of an old man in a bright green button-down at table five. Clumsily, I grab for the cubes (!), and as the old man chuckles, I blush and apologize, throwing napkins on his lap, giggling awkwardly. Old Icy Crotch winks mischievously and says, "This is the most excitement I've had before noon in a long, long time." We both laugh at the top of our lungs. I shout, "That makes two of us," and with that, my cell phone rings—that old motorcycle— suddenly, wildly, loudly revving in my pocket, as if to remind me there really are no accidents—and we burst into laughter once again.

20 City Surf

I was trying to hail a cab at the corner of Broadway and 50th, when in the ocean of yellow off-duty cabs, an old dude wearing turquoise Hawaiian print shorts appeared— riding a long skateboard— with a large white wind-sail attached to the back. He was traveling surprisingly fast and not just because it was windy. Old Dude, shirtless but wearing a helmet, was using a giant oar to "paddle" the skateboard down Broadway. As he picked up speed, he tap-tap-tapped the street more frequently with the oar, creating a perfect accidental duet with the man behind me who was playing quite beautifully, *The Godfather* theme on a rusty saxophone. Old Dude glided smoothly through rough rush hour traffic, fearless in this frenzied tide of crazy cabs and commuters. I wanted to ask Old Dude his name, the story behind the sail, and if he could give me a ride home, but I was carrying a pizza and besides, the last thing I wanted to do was break his rhythm. I'd seen a lot of oceans in my day, but I'd never seen a man ride a wave like that.

21 Must Be the Red Lipstick

Famished, I was waiting impatiently in line to order a sandwich when I noticed a messy haired little boy in front of me, seeming equally as famished and impatient. Around four years old, he was wearing a blue t-shirt and swim shorts with matching blue plastic sandals and bobbing back and forth, doing that antsy-dance that four year olds do. You know the one. Sure this dance can mean that the kid is just antsy but it can easily be confused with the I'm-about-to-pee-myself-right-now-dance. I was keeping my distance in case it was number two, or rather, the second dance, when the boy abruptly turned around and said directly to me, "Are you a mom?" "No," I said. "Do I look like a mom?" "No," he replied. "You look like a kidnapper with red lipstick on." And with that, he turned around, resumed the antsy-dance and promptly ordered a tuna sandwich.

22 Cry Later

It's a sticky afternoon in Times Square and I'm dashing to the theatre to catch the last matinee performance of *Venus in Fur*. Wet with sweat, short on time, and long on starving, I'm usually against hot dogs and other mystery foods, but it appears I'll have to make the unusual sacrifice and grab a hot dog at one of those shady street carts famous for trapping tourists into spending their last twenty bucks on overcooked salty treats on the corner of Broadway and 45th. I'm devouring the thing. It's so delicious— I'm thinking I may have misjudged hot dogs all these years—when a woman passes by with a tattoo on her arm which reads, "Cry later," in two inch cursive letters. A sign perhaps? How many days had my hot dog been smoldering sadly on those greasy metal rollers, slowly, steadily moving toward the filthy window of the cart, the way a one-eyed clown follows the woman who just can't find her car keys, slowly, steadily through the parking lot in a horror movie? Had the cart vendor worn plastic gloves when he put the dog in the bun or the bun in my hand? How many crusty Michigan fingers had actually squeezed that sticky mustard bottle? And what the hell IS a hot dog anyway? I swallowed hard and continued to the theatre, gently patting my tummy apologetically. Cry later? I just might.

23 Lullaby on the Uptown R

A rag-tag quintet of men in their mid-sixties, all wearing black fedoras, just walked onto the uptown R train and asked a blonde woman sitting alone, (sloppy ponytail, somewhere between thirty and exhausted,) if the tiny baby wrapped in a soft blue blanket on her chest was asleep. When she sadly shook her head "No," the men immediately began quietly singing, "Goodnight Sweetheart, Goodnight" in a neat, five part harmony. When the lovely rendition ended, the tired mom nodded happily and there were plenty of smiles and dollars for the crooners coming from passengers in all directions. And the baby? Sleeping peacefully.

24 Old Friends

I'm concerned about my coworker who isn't wearing his usual smile this morning. We always chat and find laughs about the little things while setting up the dining room for our business lunch crowd. New to America, my friend frequently asks me to clarify customs and expressions. But this morning we're doing our side work in silence, accompanied only by the sound of heavy silverware being dropped into the tall metal bucket as we finish polishing each piece. This strange silence has suddenly made us strangers and I'm sad about it. We're now carefully rolling silverware in white cloth napkins, which feels less like our usual "Laverne and Shirley" antics and more like a sacred religious ritual. Finally my friend whispers urgently, "I was up all night with my daughter. She is sick. Do you know this Diarrhea?" I answer in a hushed whisper, "Yes. Diarrhea and I have met quite a few times. You could say we're old friends— but I hope I never see him again!" My friend's smile returns along with a hearty laugh and the rest of our fork and knife prep is filled with talk of other old friends we'd rather not see again: Cold Sore, Pink Eye, Back Spasm, and old Charlie

Horse. Rolling silverware had never been so much fun.

25 Certain Hygienic Death

I was frantically multi-tasking as my cab jerked to a stop. These last minute emergencies included putting on lipstick, taking a work call, and paying the cab driver while opening my umbrella and door at the same time with the same hand. Half in and half out of the cab, I touched the seat to make sure I hadn't left anything behind—because I always leave something behind— and indeed, I felt something and grabbed it before realizing it was someone's cobalt blue tongue scraper, recently used. Are you familiar with tongue scrapers? They're gross, even when they belong to you. And when they don't belong to you, they are very gross. Realizing my fingers were clutching the actual scraper end, I screamed, still on the phone with my manager— who thought I was expressing outrage at being asked to work late on Friday night. I assured him I'd "happily" work the shift, and got off the phone and slammed the cab door—somewhat paralyzed—since I was somehow still clutching the enemy tongue scraper. Whose plaque and tongue-gunk was now embedded into my palm? Without thinking, I hurled the rogue tongue scraper into the air as hard as I could, accidentally hitting the cab as it drove away. When I turned toward my building, I noticed three tough guys on a bench, all wearing various articles of stone washed denim, laughing pretty hard— perhaps at my vengeance toward that innocent tongue scraper whose only real offense was being in the wrong place at the wrong time. I strutted by them, trying to play it off like, "Yeah, I always throw stuff at cars when I'm angry because I'm tough like that," when really I was thinking, "Once I get upstairs, I will immediately clean and sanitize my hand. Actually, I will boil my hand. Then I'll use the other hand to get online and purchase the largest box of plastic gloves available so that I can prevent future contamination. I will not leave my apartment until those gloves arrive. Actually, forget the glove order. I'd better not leave my apartment ever again."

26 Going Up?

I just shared an elevator with a wild-haired man dressed in a tight black suit who happened to be holding a curling iron in one hand and a rather sharp looking twelve inch sword in the other. Usually I'm excited to be in the elevator with just one other person; it's pretty rare to get on an "express" elevator in New York City. Today, I wasn't feeling that express-elevator-buzz. Instead, I wondered why I even let the doors close behind me as I stood face to face with this mysterious man who did not blink one time in four floors. As the elevator passed each floor, each "ding" was more ominous. I wasn't sure whether I was going to die or get my hair done. Pirate-Barber? Sword-Swallowing Stylist? Was this it for me? Death by sword? Or curling iron? Now I was the one not blinking as I counted two more stops until we arrived at my floor. The elevator stopped and I backed out of it keeping my eyes on him, still prepared for both makeovers and/or sword fights. Nothing happened however and status quo had never looked so gorgeous! As the doors closed behind me once again, this time

41

all I got was a delicious heart pounding rush as I heard a slow, loud laugh coming from the wild-haired elevator man, who was still going up.

27 Somebody Close

Today at work, I'm behind the bar when a nervous woman, probably around fifty, trudges in
around three pm. Heels *too* high (I've been there,) hair *too* big (I'm often there,) and eyeliner *too* heavy (I live there.) Add up all these "toos" and this equals one blind-date in my book. Sure enough, as she plops heavily onto a bar stool, she admits that she is waiting for Mr. Wonderful, or at least, Somebody Close. Even though we are indoors, she pops on a pair of sunglasses and asks for a piece of lemon to "freshen up her breath." "He'll be here any minute. He doesn't know what I look like—he might run like the wind when he sees me," she says sadly. I reply, "Whatever happens, you'll land on your feet, girl... Just be careful if you're still wearing those heels!" She laughs loudly and then immediately hunches forward and wants to know how old she "really looks." This is why I love people. A young, young woman standing nearby jumps in and says quickly, "thirty-five." I've never seen such power in a num-ber—blind-dater comes to life, sits up straight, spits out the lemon and takes off her sunglasses. Her smile is victorious as she slides off the stool to meet

her new match, a heavy set man walking toward
her, wearing a familiar nervousness in his
smile. Nine thirty pm and the pair is talking and
laughing the night away. The blind-date, is, well, out
of sight. And fifty, by the way, really does look like
thirty-five—once you kick your heels off, let your
hair down, and laugh till your eyeliner runs.

28 Paging Cyndi Lauper

I'm at the local pharmacy, comparing the "amenities" of two popular ziplock bag brands. One boasts a green "slider closure," while the rival brand features a "textured inner layer," (both guarantee to lock the freshness in!)—and JUST as I begin to chide myself for letting a simple, mundane task become a complex day-destroyer, suddenly Cyndi Lauper's "Time After Time" begins blasting from the speakers above, interrupting my plastic predicament. But this is a different version of "Time After Time." Did Lauper record the tune again recently with someone singing along in a bizarrely different key? Now I'm out of the ziplock zone and seriously pondering the likelihood of Cyndi re-recording "Time After Time," as an off-pitch duet— when, DING! It hits me: One of the *cashiers* is singing with Lauper—(passionate-shower-solo-loud)—over the intercom normally used to page employees and announce daily specials. This is wild and fantastic—a superbly off-key performance with a range of nonsensical lyric substitutions—but so full of heart and truth, it's nothing but wonderful in its awfulness. I bet this is the sort of thing that gets you fired but Cashier knows life is too short not to be outrageous. I left the pharmacy without buying ziplock bags— uncertain about why I even needed them in the first place, but certain that I could stand to be a little more outrageous, you know—time after time.

29 Shake Shake Shake

My sunny Saturday had been successful. I'd completed most of my errands before noon and was ready to head back to my apartment with two bags of groceries and a huge turquoise pillow for which I'd been saving my pennies. I guess I was in the pillow shop debating over the five shades of turquoise (mineral, aquamarine, sea-green, ocean, and peacock green,) longer than I thought because when I finally walked outside, there were what seemed like hundreds of performers covered in sequins and bright hues of satin, hustling down University Place for the NYC Dance Parade. And if there were hundreds of performers, there were thousands of onlookers hanging on barricades, excitedly watching the colorful procession. All avenue and side streets were blocked off. A few parade watchers said my only chance to cross was to walk downtown, get on the subway and exit uptown of the parade. What? With two bags of groceries and an over-sized turquoise pillow? All I really needed was to cross the street where I was standing! There were tons of officers on parade duty, so I thought I'd ask if there was a way to go through the official barriers, unofficially. Well let's just say Big Cop wouldn't give me the Little OK, so I waited for him to turn around and I made a run for it. Two other impatient crafty folks surprisingly willing to shake their moneymakers, joined me: a man on crutches and a lady pushing an empty stroller. To cross while "blending in," the three of us on sheer instinct began dancing—my grocery bags and turquoise pillow, his crutches, her stroller—we put all the props together and did a little impromptu dance number, keeping rhythm with the dancers around us. So why did the groceries, the pillow, the crutches, and the stroller cross the road? You know: to get to the other side.

30 Lisa Finds Liza

When I'm thrift shopping at my special spot in
Chelsea, I often run into a talented drag performer
I've seen on the NYC circuit. She always arches
her eyebrow flirtatiously when she sees me. We
always reach quickly for the same vintage
dresses— but she gets them first, simply because
her arms are longer. We're friendly about the
simultaneous dress-grabbing. We're forever
winking, nodding and mmmhmm-ing at each other,
even though Long Arms usually scores the best
stuff. But today, I hit the Vintage Diva Jackpot when
I dove for a Liza Minelli album, "Live at the Olympia
in Paris," which had been propped in the back of a
deep bin of pillows. Timing is everything, (especially
when you're dealing with a capital D diva like Long
Arms,) so I knew I'd need to actually dive into the
bin to earn that album, risking a possible lice
situation. The dive was successful, (and bug free,
thank goodness.) I took a deep breath and cradled
the album in my arms—this was probably the closest I'd ever come to hugging Liza. Long Arms broke
my Minelli trance with a loud, "Stop it!," then
grinned and said, "Well... it should be yours

because there's something very Liza about you.
What's your name, anyway?" "Lisa," I said, smiling.
"Lisa, with an 'S'."

31 Kinda Psycho

I'm showering at the gym and there's a woman
gossiping in the stall behind me to someone in the
stall behind her. Her juicy chatter flows as steadily
as the steam from the shower. I mean, she never
stops talking. Shower Catty topic-hops by listing
juicy life events which sound like too-long titles of
cheap novels ranging from: "My Secret Feelings
For David, My Dry Cleaner," to "His Mustache Intox-
icates Me Like A Cheap Chardonnay." She's pretty
much covering all bases— if you know what I
mean. I'm absorbing this trash talk like a curious
sponge but when I leave the stall, I learn that
Shower Catty is talking to no one at all. The water
is running but there's no one in that stall behind her.
Did someone get good (and clean) fed-up and
leave in between tawdry titles or had she been
alone the entire time? As I blow-dry my hair, I'm
considering all possible explanations when
suddenly the hair dryer next to me turns on by itself.
Using the mirror, I look behind me—halfway expect-
ing a man with a melted face or perhaps a hockey
mask covering a melted face, to be looking back at
me. Deciding that leaving with wet hair would be

infinitely better than starring in my own horror flick possibly called, *Last Moments in the Locker Room*, I turn and basically run toward the exit. It dawns on me as I'm hurrying home that it's Friday the thirteenth and I'm chuckling about the coincidence when I suddenly run smack into an old flame, which actually takes the cake for spookiest event of the night. Saturday the fourteenth, I love you madly.

32 Deli Makeover

Crazy-late for a late-in-the-day meeting and apparently more crazy about cosmetics, I just re-applied my makeup from start to finish in the middle of the deli on 6th Avenue near Hudson. I used the top of a freezer full of Haagen Dazs as my counter in an aisle between the Pringles and the Ajax. I'm not talking about a quick lipstick re-application. I'm talking about blending two shades of foundation and adding blush, eye shadow, eye liner, eye brow gel, mascara, lipstick, lipliner, bronzer, and powder. I'm talking brushes, a few q-tips, six or seven glittery palettes, and a travel magnifying mirror with three shiny panels that can be propped open on most anything, including an industrial ice cream freezer. This kind of aesthetic artistry is usually only seen at the counter in Bloomingdales, plus the fragrance testers, minus the Drano selection. The best part about this maquillage menagerie? Deli employees didn't say a word or make a move to stop my makeup madness! Because, my kind of crazy? You just can't make that up!

33 The Right Stuff

Sitting by the pool, I noticed an older red-haired woman wrapping a large Spider-Man towel around her sandy-haired grandson, who was probably around four or five years old. He was dripping and shivering and she was hustling to keep him warm and find his clothing, all at once. You could tell that Grandma wasn't the usual pick-up person. She was zipping and unzipping each zipper on a green backpack as if she'd look for something and then forget what she was looking for and then look for something else and then forget that thing. My heart went out to her as the boy grew a little more impatient with each zip. He took his swimsuit off and handed it to Grandma to speed the process, but this made matters worse because now she wasn't sure where to put the wet suit. You could just tell she was thinking, "I'm not the right person for this job." As she bent over the backpack, like someone checking oil under a car hood, she unearthed a spoon, some sort of action figure missing an arm, and finally a dry pair of Spider-Man underwear for the soggy boy. She tossed him the underwear and seemed to be gaining confidence as she began sorting through clothing and toys in and out of the bag. "This is the wet stuff," she said, making a pile. "This is the dry stuff," she said, as she made another pile. "And this is the NAKED STUFF," the boy yelled, and with that, he shook his naked stuff back and forth in front of his very shocked Grandma. I stifled a laugh and Grandma looked up at me and we chimed in unison, "Boys will be boys!"

34 Magic Carpet

I was in a hurry walking to work— juggling my
purse on one shoulder and my heavy work shoes in
a cloth bag on the other—feeling genuinely
surprised at the spring in my step. I wasn't usually
this cheerful on my way to bartend for seven hours,
but there was something in the air. I was almost
whistling and I hated whistling. Enjoying this
newfound energy, I tried to take in everything
around me as I walked—the faces of the people I
passed and the beauty of the great blue sky— then
suddenly I couldn't see a thing. A light gray rug had
accidentally fallen from a fire escape on Avenue C
and landed on my head, closing out completely my
enjoyable view. What were the chances of a rug
landing on your head if you weren't a balding man?
I panicked a little. Unfortunately, it was one of those
bathroom rugs that wrap around your toilet which
meant there were most likely toilet type thingies lin-
gering on it! Unmentionables. Unimaginables! As I
ripped the rug off my head and shook my hair out
while gagging, almost immediately an older lady
yelled down in a thick Italian accent, "It's clean! It's
very, very cleeeeeeean!" I took a step back and

hurled it in the air so that it reached the tiny hands of the woman leaning out the window. She caught it and said, "You are good lady!," and I couldn't help grinning as I turned around and headed back to work. Usually the rug is pulled out from under you, but I guess if it's dropped on your head and the rug is clean— that's a good thing.

35 Trash Boss

Waiting to cross the street, on the corner of Avenue B and 14th, I noticed a silver haired woman wearing a sharp red blazer with a gold decorative anchor pinned to the lapel, navy blue slacks, and white shoes. She was perched on the edge of a green metal trash container, puffing away on a thick expensive-looking cigar, while reading the name and address on a huge priority mail package— out loud— in a smoky voice. I looked around but no one crossing the street or hanging out nearby moved to claim the empty package. The germa-phobe in me flinched. Who perches on the edge of a trash can? This was serious dedication to im-prove recycling in the neighborhood— and Trash Boss seemed cool with the challenge. She caught me staring as I passed by. She leaned over, blew some smoke in my direction, and said confidently, "My business is this block, honey. I keep an eye on things. I decide what's garbage." She looked me up and down, deciding I must have been all right— thankfully—and puffed on her cigar once again as I crossed the street and waved a hasty goodbye. I think I just met a real gangster.

36 Piece of Cake

It's Taco Tuesday and I'm at my local taco spot
waiting for my order. There are two goth looking
tweens behind me in line and they are the epitome
of New York Cool. I'm three times their age and
won't achieve their level of cool in my lifetime
because this cool is the kind you're born with; you
can't generate it. I'm lost in the sudden grief of this
unreachable coolness, vowing to at least try black
lipstick the next time I pick up my tacos, when the
tween with blue hair taps my shoulder and says,
"You've got cake, girl." I swallow nervously and
reply, "Like I eat too much cake?" The other tween,
wearing forty or fifty safety pins on a torn black
t-shirt, steps up and says quickly, "No, you're all
good in the back. You've got cake." Relief! My
backside has passed some sort of tweenage cool-
test! And cool things are called "cake" now and you
bet your buns I can roll with that! Am I cooler than I
thought? Just to see if I can talk the cake-talk, I say
in the coolest voice I can muster, "So, cake is good,
right?" "Yep," the first tween nods and the second
tween smiles and says, "Cake is good."

37 Sometimes You Feel Like A...

Starving, I ducked into a corner store on 12th and 8th, grabbed a package of almonds, threw a couple bucks on the counter and hastily started tearing at the bag while waiting for my change. Somehow during the hasty tearing, the bag popped and for a few seconds, it rained almonds—showering all shoppers standing in line to pay, including an elderly woman comparing pears and three men in white aprons behind the counter— presumably the actual brothers referenced on the awning outside of the deli, which reads, "Three Brothers." Oh, there were almonds in the cash drawer, almonds in the pastry case, and almonds in the rocker-looking bangs of the woman behind me. My first instinct was to shout a general apology over the mayhem but then my laughter took over which is not unusual for me in embarrassing situations. So this was the picture: me scooting around the deli snort-laughing and gathering almonds from the most unlikely places. I reached into the cash drawer (a no-no,) basically swept the floor with my purse (eww,) and extracted a single almond from the bangs of the woman behind me (inappropriate.) Still hungry but too embarrassed to buy a second bag of almonds from the three glaring siblings, I bought a bag from the deli down the block instead, and waited until I was safely outside to open it.

38 Greek Drama

I just ran into a very stern purple-bearded man who nudged me with his paper-mache trident as I tried to squeeze by him to cross the street. Our eyes met and my first instinct was to giggle because when was the last time anyone was poked by a three pronged spear? What year was this? Any instinct to chortle however was completely squelched by the serious look on Purple Beard's face. He growled without moving a muscle in his face and said, "I'm sorry. I've got to get through here. I'm late and I don't think anyone realizes how tricky it is to commute with a trident." I nodded, eyes wide, smiling cheerfully as I let Purple Beard pass me. His walk was strangely majestic. He looked like he'd just sashayed out of a punk-rock Greek play and landed smack in the middle of rush hour traffic on Broadway and 27th. Had I almost been lanced by some sad spoiled King who was just trying to get back to the Acropolis or was it just time for coffee?

39 Fitting Room Blues

I'm holed up in a Macy's fitting room surrounded by
blue jeans— straight leg, curvy fit, flare, boot cut,
tailored, embellished, boyfriend, skinny, trouser,
and low-rise. Despite the range of styles and sizes I
have single-handedly lugged into this tiny over-lit
fitting room, not a single pair fits correctly. I'm about
to give up, so I'm sort of squatting and staring at the
denim mountain I've named "DesPair." I like each
and every one of these pairs of jeans but they sure
don't like me! It's a conspiracy! What did I ever do
to these jeans? I've never met a single pair of these
particular jeans and yet somehow each pair has
deliberately reflected or revealed one of my known
or unknown imperfections. My belly practically folds
over the waist in this pair! These are too tight on my
calves! This pair makes me look like I have an
additional knee above my knee! Mid-breakdown,
I'm trying on the mid-rise jeans when Gloria the
saleswoman, gently knocks and asks if I'd like to try
the "relaxed fit." I know what she's trying to do. She
wants me to know, that she knows, that I'm
cracking up in here—because maybe she
overheard me voicing theories of conspiracy

regarding the duplicity of this denim. In a quiet, silky voice, she asks if I need anything. (For the record, Gloria has been gliding through the fitting room hallway in jeans that positively sing her praises so loudly that I can practically hear "Hallelujah!" each time I catch a glimpse of her from the crack in my door, so no, she's not getting my jean-rage.) "What I really need now, Gloria, is a Twinkie. And a glass of wine," I say calmly. Smooth Gloria doubles over in laughter and I see that her belly sort of folds over the waist of her perfect jeans and this gives me some hope. Maybe I've been too hard on these blue jeans. Maybe I've been too hard on myself. I think it's time to put my sweatpants back on and call it a day.

40 Life Tips

My heart pretty much melted last night when a spirited woman wearing a Dolly Parton hairdo and tons of eighties glamour make-up, wanted to pay for a beer with a pair of pink, dangly rhinestone earrings— instead of cash. She tapped on the bar with purple nails and said she thought the exchange was a fair one. Since it seemed as if I too was the, "kind of lady who treasured fake gems," I accepted the compliment and stuffed a few bills from my tip jar (for her beer) into the cash register and then put the earrings on. She sipped her beer knowingly and said, squinting through long false eyelashes, "You never lose for askin'." I nodded and checked my reflection in the dusty mirror behind the bar, enjoying how much those dangly pink rhinestones sparkled when they caught the light.

41 Middle-Aged Math

Just auditioned as "Mom" with two girls, five and seven years old. Once I knew their ages, they wanted to know mine. "Ok," I said, "Add five and seven." They shrieked in unison, "You're twelve?!" "No," I said, "Now multiply three times twelve." "You're thirty-six!," yelled the seven year old. "Now subtract six," I said, quickly. A little time passed as they used their fingers and whispered together. "You're thirty!," they squealed together again. "Kind of around there—for today," I said, smiling. The seven year old jumped up, rapidly flapping the paper containing her lines and said, "Oh, because that's what the page says, right?!" Catching on quickly, the five year old squealed, "Yes, the page says the Mom has to be in her thirties so you have to be WHAT THE PAGE SAYS!" "Yes, girls," I said grinning, "What the page says."

42 We're All Weirdos Anyway

Taking the 5 train home, I looked up from my book and noticed a tall tan man in a towering cowboy hat sitting across from me, staring at a young lavender haired woman next to him who was engrossed in her phone. With the curiosity of a child, he seemed fascinated with her purple locks. My guess was there weren't many lavender haired cowgirls where he came from. Meanwhile I was sorta staring at his giant cowboy hat, the largest I'd ever seen, which seemed way more out of place on a NYC subway than violet-hued hair. He looked over at me and subtlety pointed to the lavender haired woman, his face like a boy seeing a matchbox truck for the first time, mouth slightly open, eyes glazed. He mouthed the words, "That hair," and I nodded and pointed to his hat and mouthed the words, "That hat." He got it right away and boy did he laugh as he tipped that big ol' hat in my direction as I chuckled in a good clean fun sort of way. Lavender Hair, still oddly entranced by her phone, was none the wiser, but Cowboy had learned that there's room enough for everybody on the NYC subway.

43 Cheese Burger Medium

It's eleven am and I'm having a late breakfast at my favorite dingy diner in Alphabet City. A woman with yellow curlers in her hair, somewhere in her sixties, stumbles in through the front screen door, dressed monochromatically in various shades of yellow. She pushes a red shopping cart, the contents of which are unknown since everything inside is carefully wrapped in black garbage bags. She's huffing and puffing as she grabs a newspaper and pushes her cart past the host trying to seat her. The mysterious items must be highly precious because Yellow Curlers abruptly parks her cart *behind* the counter. Still behind the counter, she rings the bell, taps the top of the cash register and shouts, "I need a cheese burger and a Coke! Please and thank you! It's been a rocky mountain morning! Cheese burger medium!" The grill man nods, the waitress shrugs, the host gestures for Yellow Curlers to seat herself, and I promptly order another cup of coffee.

44 New Yorkers Crossing

I was crossing the crowded intersection at 47th and 8th Avenue, and apparently our little pedestrian group wasn't moving fast enough for a sweaty cab driver. He tried to cut around us while throwing his arms in the air yelling, "Move! Move! Move!" Without thinking, I pointed to the walk sign, smiled and yelled back, "We got the WALK, baby!" Immediately, three or four of my fellow pedestrians yelled, "YEAH, BABY!" It was the perfect chorus to my sudden solo, and in flawless New York rhythm we basically sauntered as a group to the corner, chuckling confidently. As the cab driver peeled away, he threw his arms in the air again—but not in anger— this time he was laughing right along with us.

45 Lady Luck Meets Whiskey River

This morning a whiskered old man in a long, tattered black coat and red mittens asked me for one dollar at the corner of Broadway and 50th. "I'm going to Whiskey River," he explained politely, his voice as tired as an old dirt road. Chuckling, I said, "Don't you need more than a dollar to get to Whiskey River nowadays?" He flashed a toothless smile and said, "I gotta be honest with you, pretty lady. I'm already halfway there." As I reached in my coat pocket, I saw that he was telling the truth. There was whiskey in his eyes and sadness on his breath. I handed him a dollar, wondering how he got to this place—half-drunk but whole-clever at 50th Street on this frigid Thursday morning in December. Old Whiskers took the money and said, "Thank you, Lady Luck," before bowing slightly and scurrying quickly down Broadway, his red mittened hands clasped behind his back. I watched him disappear into a crowd of people in brightly covered coats taking pictures of each other and laughing. Although a trip to Whiskey River was tempting— I headed to the deli for a coffee instead, grinning ear to ear all the way there.

ABOUT LISA HICKMAN

LISA HICKMAN IS A NYC BASED ACTOR, SINGER, WRITER, VOICE OVER ARTIST AND TEACHER. HER ONE WOMAN CABARET SHOW, "JACKPOT," ORIGINATED AND RAN AT THE DUPLEX IN GREENWICH VILLAGE. LISA HAS PERFORMED ALL OVER NYC IN VENUES INCLUDING: DIXON PLACE, GALAPAGOS, H.E.R.E., EXPANDED ARTS, D.U.M.B.O., THE BUSHWICK STARR, THEATER FOR THE NEW CITY, THE WHITNEY MUSEUM AT ALTRIA, AXIS THEATRE COMPANY, ROOM 53, AND THE TANK. SHE TOURED NATIONALLY WITH TYLER PERRY IN *I CAN DO BAD ALL BY MYSELF* AND IS FEATURED IN NUMEROUS INDEPENDENT FILMS AND COMMERCIALS. TV CREDITS INCLUDE *ORANGE IS THE NEW BLACK* AND *THE PERFECT MURDER*. LISA GRADUATED FROM BROOKLYN COLLEGE WITH AN M.F.A. IN ACTING AND PACE UNIVERSITY WITH A B.F.A. IN ACTING. SHE STUDIES ACTING AT HB STUDIO AND VOICE WITH HELEN GALLAGHER. SHE IS AN ADJUNCT PROFESSOR AT PACE UNIVERSITY, SUB-INSTRUCTOR AT PLAYWRIGHTS HORIZONS THEATER SCHOOL, AND HEADS FRESHMAN DRAMA AT XAVIER HIGH SCHOOL. MORE ABOUT LISA'S ADVENTURES AT WWW.LISAHICKMAN.COM